Ninja Foodi Smart XL Grill Cookbook for Beginners

550 Quick, Easy and Delicious Recipes for Indoor Grilling and Air Frying (Beginners and Advanced Users)

Kelly Brainerd

© **Copyright 2020 - All rights reserved.**

The content contained within this book may not be reproduced, duplicated or transmitted without direct written permission from the author or the publisher.

Under no circumstances will any blame or legal responsibility be held against the publisher, or author, for any damages, reparation, or monetary loss due to the information contained within this book, either directly or indirectly.

Legal Notice:

This book is copyright protected. It is only for personal use. You cannot amend, distribute, sell, use, quote or paraphrase any part, or the content within this book, without the consent of the author or publisher.

Disclaimer Notice:

Please note the information contained within this document is for educational and entertainment purposes only. All effort has been executed to present accurate, up to date, reliable, complete information. No warranties of any kind are declared or implied. Readers acknowledge that the author is not engaged in the rendering of legal, financial, medical or professional advice. The content within this book has been derived from various sources. Please consult a licensed professional before attempting any techniques outlined in this book.

By reading this document, the reader agrees that under no circumstances is the author responsible for any losses, direct or indirect, that are incurred as a result of the use of the information contained within this document, including, but not limited to, errors, omissions, or inaccuracies.

Table of Contents

Introduction 7

    What is the Ninja Foodi Smart XL Grill? 7

    What are its Features and Functions? 7

    Cleaning Your Ninja Foodi Smart XL Grill 8

    Cooking Tips and Tricks 10

Chapter 1: Breakfast Recipes 13

    Amazing Tater Tots Eggs 13

    Delicious Rum Sundae 14

    Honey and Coconut Medley 15

    Baked Muffin Egg 16

    French Burrito 17

    Sweet BBQ Chicken 18

    Crispy Mac and Cheese 19

    French Toasties 21

Chapter 2: Chicken and Poultry Recipes 22

    Special Taste of Alfredo Chicken 22

    Spitting Paprika Chicken 23

    Magical Coconut Touched Chicken 24

    Herbed Up Roast Chicken 25

Wonderful Tangy Orange Chicken 26

Easy Lemon Mustard Chicken 27

Teriyaki Chicken 28

Italian Chicken Skewers 29

California Grilled Chicken 30

Sweet Chili-Lime Grilled Chicken 31

Honey Balsamic Grilled Chicken Thighs 32

Chapter 3: Beef and Red Meat Recipes 34

Delicious Cheeseburger 34

Grilled Steak and Salad 35

Homely Honey Ham 36

Bacon-Wrapped Up Pork Loin 37

Italian Meatballs 38

Different Pork Sandwich 39

Peppers & Sausage 40

Beef Stroganoff 42

Crusted Steak 43

Bourbon Pork Chops 44

Fleshed Out Onion Beef Roast 45

Fried Potatoes and Pork Cutlets 46

Bacon-wrapped Pork 47

Grilled Steak with Dry Chili Dipping Sauce 48

Memphis-Style Dry Ribs 49

Chapter 4: Vegetarian and Vegan Recipes 51

Feisty Avocado Toast 51

Mexican Corn 52

Balsamic Tomatoes Roast 53

Spicy Broccoli Medley 54

Super Garlic Potatoes 55

Roasted Potatoes and Fancy Asparagus 56

Cheesy Zucchini Love 58

Lemon Pepper Brussels Sprouts 59

Spiced Up Chickpeas 60

Chapter 5: Fish & Seafood Recipes 61

Southern Catfish 61

Fried Prawns 63

Gouache Prawns 64

Mediterranean Sea Bream 65

Air Crisped Salmon 66

Broiled Tilapia 67

Air Catfish 68

Tuna Patties 69

Chili Lime Tilapia 70

Breaded Shrimp 71

Chapter 6: Snacks and Appetizers Recipes 72

Chicken with Herbs and Cream 72

Meaty Bratwursts 73

Delicious Taco Cups 74

Mustard and Veggie 75

Season Garlic Carrots 77

Sausage Patties 78

Cute Mozarella Bites 79

Simple Garlic Bread 79

Particularly Crispy Tomatoes 81

Fancy Baked Apples 82

Chapter 7: Desserts Recipes 83

Grilled Fruit Skewers 83

Chocolate Marshmallow Banana 84

Grilled Donut Ice Cream Sandwich 85

Bloomin' Grilled Apples 86

S'mores Roll-Up 87

Grilled Pineapple Sundaes 88

Conclusion 89

Introduction

What is the Ninja Foodi Smart XL Grill?

Ninja Foodi Smart XL Grill with 4-Quart Air Fry and Smart Cook System. It has taken the cooking world by storm and is considered to be a significant breakthrough in the cooking world and the ultimate solution for all your cooking needs in one Smart device. It has combined 6 cooking functions - grill, air crisp, bake, roast, broil, dehydrate in one compact device that can be used both indoor and outdoor. It is virtually considered to be smoke-free and provides the user with a fresh aroma and reserved taste and nutrition of the Ingredients: included in the food. It comes with a kitchen thermometer, which helps a lot in giving the right heating to your food to achieve the perfect crisp and tenderness. The features and functions of the Ninja Foodi Smart XL Grill will be covered in the coming portions.

What are its Features and Functions?

The Ninja Foodi Smart XL Grill is one of the most competent and state of the art cooking appliance. It comes with the most modern and user-friendly features. These features include:

- Ninja Foodi Smart XL Grill with Smart Cook System. Smart Cook System—4 smart protein settings, 9 customizable doneness levels, and the Foodi Smart Thermometer enable you to achieve the perfect doneness from rare to well done at the touch of a button. No more guesswork and no more under or over cooking

- XL Capacity—grill 50% more food than the original Ninja Foodi Grill for delicious family sized meals. Grill grate fits up to 6 steaks, up to 24 hot dogs, mains and sides at the same time, and more

- Air fry crisp with up to 75% less fat than deep frying (tested against hand cut, deep fried French fries), using the included 4 qt crisper basket

- Unique Smoke Control System—the combination of our chef recommended grilling practices, a temperature-controlled grill grate, splatter shield, and cool air zone reduces smoke, keeping it out of the kitchen

- Forgot to defrost dinner? Transform foods from frozen to perfectly char grilled in under 25 minutes

- Dual Sensor Foodi Smart Thermometer—continuously monitors temperature in two places for even more accurate results. Multi task with peace of mind as food cooks to perfection

The primary cooking functions that are included in the Ninja Foodi Smart XL Grill include 6 cooking functions - grill, air crisp, bake, roast, broil, dehydrate. It can also perform sautéing, simmering, and pressure cooking for letting you prepare your food with the utmost care and preservation of the aroma and taste of the Ingredients.

Cleaning Your Ninja Foodi Smart XL Grill

It might appear very tricky to thoroughly clean the Ninja Foodi Smart XL Grill, but it is not complicated at all. You merely need to follow certain easy steps, and your device is ready to go for another round. It is recommended to thoroughly clean the Ninja Foodi Smart XL Grill after every use. To clean the unit thoroughly and safely, follow the following guidelines:

- Let the device cool down before cleaning.

- Unplug the device from the power source.

- For quick cooling, keep the hood of the device open.

- The grill gate, splatter shield, crisper basket, cooking pot, cleaning brush, and the rest of the accessories are certified as **DISHWASHER SAFE**.
- The thermometer is not dishwasher safe.
- Rinse the accessories like splatter shield, grill gate, etc. for better cleaning results.
- Use the cleaning brush included with the device for handwashing.
- For cleaning baked-on cheese or sauces, utilize the other end of the cleaning brush for being used as a scrapper for effective hand washing.
- Either towel-dry or air-dry all the components after hand washing.
- **DO NOT** dip the main unit in any liquid, including water.
- **DO NOT** use any rasping cleaners or tools.
- **NEVER** use any sort of liquid cleaning solution near or on the thermometer.
- Always use a cotton swab or compressed air to avoid any damage to the jack.

In case of any grease or food residue left and stuck on the components of the Ninja Foodi Smart XL Grill, follow the following cleaning steps thoroughly:

1. If the residue is stuck on the splatter shield, grill gate, or any other accessory or part, soak it in warm soapy water solution before cleaning.

2. The splatter should be cleaned thoroughly after every use. For better cleansing, soak it in warm water overnight will assists efficiently in softening the stuck grease or sauces.

3. You can also deep clean the splatter shield by thoroughly immersing it in water and further boiling it for approximately 10 minutes.

4. Moreover, you can then rinse it effectively with room temperature water and let it dry properly for better results.

For deep cleaning the thermometer, you can soak both the silicone grip and the stainless steel tip in a container full of warm water. But, keep in mind that the jack or the cord **SHOULD NOT** be immersed or soaked in any solution, including water, as mentioned earlier. The thermometer holder of the Ninja Foodi Smart XL Grill is clearly **HANDWASH** only.

Cooking Tips and Tricks

The Ninja Foodi Smart XL Grill is the ultimate solution for your kitchen, provided that you master the art of using it like a pro. For mastering this ultimate cooking device, use the following tips and tricks, and yield the best possible results. These tips and tricks are going to give your cooking a new touch of ultimate taste, crispiness, and aroma. These include the following:

Air Crisp

- Coating your veggies thoroughly and evenly with a little oil prior to air crisping them will get you better crispiness. For consistent and effective browning of your food, thoroughly arrange all the Ingredients: as much evenly as possible in the Cook & Crisp basket.

Steam

- Steam your vegetables in the Cook & Crisp basket for giving them an extra layer of texture. Furthermore, toss them thoroughly with oil and then perfectly Air Crisp them with the crisping lid.

Pressure

- Always use hot water when you are pressure cooking your food. This will help you Ninja Foodi Smart XL Grill build pressure much faster.

Broil

- Broiling can be effectively used as a second step in thoroughly combo-cooking your meals with the ultimate crispiness. Have a sneak and peak at your food throughout to have a better idea of having even crispiness of the Ingredients.

Roast and Bake

- Instead of the baking dish, go for the Ninja Multi-purpose Pan for effective baking instead of the regular baking pan.

Sautéing or Searing

- The sauté or sear function can be efficiently used, just like the stovetop. You should always use the LO function for simmering, the MED function for through sautéing, and the HIGH function for searing or boiling various meats.

- You should efficiently sear your food before slow cooking or pressure cooking to build the flavor as well as caramelization in your favorite food.

- Leave your meats 20 to 30 minutes at room temperature before searing them. You should also pat dry them thoroughly before searing them, in addition to keeping them at room temperature prior to searing.

Dehydrate

- Always pat your food as much dry as possible before placing them in the Cook & Crisp Basket.

- You can put the Ingredients: like veggies and fruits closer and flat to have more space, but they should not be stacked or overlapped at all.

- Almost all fruits and veggies take around 6 to 8 hours to dehydrate, while jerky is known to take 5 to 7 hours for thorough dehydration. The longer the dehydration time, the better and crispier your food will be.

- The Roast function should be used for approximately 1 minute at 330 degrees Fahrenheit to thoroughly pasteurize Ingredients. This function should be sued when you are using dehydrated meats and fish in your recipe.

Chapter 1: Breakfast Recipes

Amazing Tater Tots Eggs

Prep time: 5-10 minutes

Cooking time: 25 minutes

Servings: 4

Ingredients:

- 1 pound frozen tater tots
- 1 cup cheddar cheese, shredded
- 2 sausages, cooked and sliced
- Cooking spray as needed
- Salt and pepper to taste
- ¼ cup milk
- 5 whole eggs

Directions:

1. Preheat your Ninja Foodi Smart XL Grill in Bake mode at 390 degrees F for 3 minutes
2. Take a bowl and add eggs, milk, season with salt and pepper
3. Take a small baking pan and grease with oil
4. Add egg mix to the pan and transfer to your Foodi
5. Cook for 5 minutes, place sausages on top of eggs, sprinkle cheese on top
6. Bake for 20 minutes more
7. Serve and enjoy!

Nutritional Information Per Serving:

Calories: 187, Fat: 8 g, Saturated Fat: 3 g, Carbohydrates: 21 g, Fiber: 1 g, Sodium: 338 mg, Protein: 9 g

Delicious Rum Sundae

Prep time: 5-10 minutes

Cooking time: 8 minutes

Servings: 4

Ingredients:

- ½ cup dark rum
- ½ cup brown sugar, packed
- 1 teaspoon cinnamon, ground
- 1 pineapple, cored and sliced
- Vanilla ice cream for serving

Directions:

1. Take a large-sized bowl and add sugar, rum, and cinnamon
2. Add pineapple in the layer, dredge them, and coat well
3. Preheat your Smart XL Grill to MAX and set the timer to 8 minutes
4. Once you hear the beep, strain any rum from pineapple slices and transfer them to the grill grate
5. Cook for 6-8 minutes; cook in batches if needed
6. Top each ring with a scoop of ice cream and sprinkle cinnamon
7. Enjoy!

Nutritional Information Per Serving:

Calories: 240, Fat: 4 g, Saturated Fat: 1 g, Carbohydrates: 43 g, Fiber: 8 g, Sodium: 85 mg, Protein: 2 g

Honey and Coconut Medley

Prep time: 5-10 minutes

Cooking time: 10-308 minutes

Servings: 4

Ingredients:

- Baking paper as needed
- ¼ ice cream sorbet
- 1 tablespoon lemon juice
- 1 tablespoon honey
- ½ small, fresh pineapples

Directions:

1. Preheat your Ninja Foodi Smart XL Grill to 392 degrees F in "AIR CRISP" mode; line the bottom of the basket with baking paper

2. Cut pineapple lengthwise into eight pieces, remove the peel with eyes alongside the woody trunk

3. Take a bowl and mix in lemon juice and honey, brush pineapple pieces with the mixture. Transfer to the basket. Sprinkle coconut over it

4. Push to Air Fryer and cook for 12 minutes

5. Serve and enjoy some ice cream.

6. Enjoy!

Nutritional Information Per Serving:

Calories: 435, Fat: 16 g, Saturated Fat: 4 g, Carbohydrates: 61 g, Fiber: 2 g, Sodium: 85 mg, Protein: 9 g

Baked Muffin Egg

(Prep time: 5-10 minutes\ Cooking time: 15 minutes |For 4 servings)

Ingredients:

- Parsley, chopped as needed
- Salt and pepper to taste
- 4 large eggs
- 4 large bell peppers, seeded and tops removed
- 4 bacon, sliced, cooked, and chopped
- 1 cup cheddar cheese, shredded

Directions:

1. Take your bell peppers and divide cheese and bacon between them, crack an egg into each of the bell peppers. Season them with salt and pepper

2. Preheat Ninja Foodi Smart XL Grill by pressing the "AIR CRISP" option and setting it to "390 Degrees F" and timer to 15 minutes

3. Let it preheat until you hear a beep

4. Transfer bell pepper to your cooking basket and transfer to Foodi Grill, lock lid, and cook for 10-15 minutes until egg whites are cooked well until the yolks are slightly runny

5. Remove peppers from the basket and garnish with parsley, serve and enjoy!

Nutritional Information Per Serving:

Calories: 326, Fat: 23 g, Saturated Fat: 10 g, Carbohydrates: 10 g, Fiber: 2 g, Sodium: 781 mg, Protein: 22 g

French Burrito

Prep time: 5-10 minutes

Cooking time: 5 minutes

Servings: 2

Ingredients:

- 2 tortillas
- ½ cup bacon, cooked crisp and crumbled
- ½ cup cheddar cheese, shredded
- 2 whole eggs, scrambled

Directions:

1. Take a bowl and add eggs, bacon, and cheese
2. Top tortillas with the mix
3. Roll the tortillas, transfer to the Ninja Foodi Smart XL Grill
4. Select AIR CRISP and cook for 5 minutes at 250 degrees F
5. Serve and enjoy!

Nutritional Information Per Serving:

Calories: 531, Fat: 15 g, Saturated Fat: 3 g, Carbohydrates: 81 g, Fiber: 2 g, Sodium: 1125 mg, Protein: 18 g

Sweet BBQ Chicken

Prep time: 5-10 minutes

Cooking time: 40 minutes

Servings: 4

Ingredients:

- Salt and pepper to taste
- 1 cup white vinegar
- ¾ cup onion, chopped
- ¼ cup tomato paste
- ¼ cup garlic, minced
- 1 cup of water
- 1 cup of soy sauce
- ¾ cup of sugar
- 6 chicken drumsticks

Directions:

1. Take a Ziploc bag and add all Ingredients: to it
2. Marinate for at least 2 hours in your refrigerator
3. Insert the crisper basket, and close the hood
4. Preheat Ninja Foodi Smart XL Grill by pressing the "AIR CRISP" option at 390 degrees F for 40 minutes
5. Place the grill pan accessory in the air fryer
6. Flip the chicken after every 10 minutes
7. Take a saucepan and pour the marinade into it, and heat over medium flame until sauce thickens
8. Brush with the glaze
9. Serve warm and enjoy!

Nutritional Information Per Serving:

Calories: 460, Fat: 20 g, Saturated Fat: 5 g, Carbohydrates: 26 g, Fiber: 3 g, Sodium: 126 mg, Protein: 28 g

Crispy Mac and Cheese

Prep time: 5-10 minutes

Cooking time: 10 minutes

Servings: 4

Ingredients:

- 1 tablespoon parmesan cheese, grated
- Salt and pepper to taste
- 1 and ½ cheddar cheese, grated
- ½ cup warmed milk
- ½ cup broccoli
- 1 cup elbow macaroni

Directions:

1. Preheat Ninja Foodi Smart XL Grill by pressing the "AIR CRISP" option and setting it to "400 Degrees F" and timer to 10 minutes

2. let it preheat until you hear a beep

3. Take a pot and add water, allow it to boil

4. Add macaroni and veggies and broil for about 10 minutes until the mixture is Al Dente

5. Drain the pasta and vegetables

6. Toss the pasta and veggies with cheese

7. Season with some pepper and salt and transfer the mixture to your Foodi

8. Sprinkle some more parmesan on top and cook for about 15 minutes.

9. Allow it to cool for about 10 minutes once done

10. Enjoy!

Nutritional Information Per Serving:

Calories: 180, Fat: 11 g, Saturated Fat: 3 g, Carbohydrates: 14 g, Fiber: 3 g, Sodium: 287 mg, Protein: 6 g

French Toasties

Prep time: 5-10 minutes

Cooking time: 10 minutes

Servings: 4

Ingredients:

- Cooking spray as needed
- 6 slices bread, sliced into strips
- ¼ teaspoon vanilla extract
- ¼ teaspoon ground cinnamon
- ¼ cup granulated sugar
- ½ cup milk
- 4 whole eggs

Directions:

1. Take a bowl and beat in eggs, milk
2. Stir in sugar, vanilla, and cinnamon
3. Dip the bread in the mix
4. Preheat your Ninja Foodi Smart XL Grill in AIR CRISP for 10 minutes at 400 degrees F
5. Transfer bread to the Foodi and cook for 3-5 minutes per side
6. Enjoy!

Nutritional Information Per Serving:

Calories: 183, Fat: 6 g, Saturated Fat: 2 g, Carbohydrates: 24 g, Fiber: 3 g, Sodium: 269 mg, Protein: 9 g

Chapter 2: Chicken and Poultry Recipes

Special Taste of Alfredo Chicken

Prep time: 5-10 minutes

Cooking time: 20 minutes

Servings: 4

Ingredients:

- 1 large apple, wedged
- 1 tablespoon lemon juice
- 4 chicken breasts, halved
- 4 teaspoons chicken seasoning
- 4 slices provolone cheese
- ¼ cup blue cheese, crumbled
- ½ cup alfredo sauce

Directions:

1. Take a mixing bowl and add seasoning
2. Take another bowl and toss apple with lemon juice
3. Set your Ninja Foodi Smart XL Grill to Grill and MED mode, set timer to 16 minutes
4. Transfer chicken over grill grate, lock lid, and cook for 8 minutes
5. Flip and cook for 8 minutes more
6. Grill the apple in a similar manner, 2 minutes per side
7. Serve the cooked chicken with sauce, grilled apple, and cheese
8. Enjoy!

Nutritional Information Per Serving:

Calories: 247, Fat: 19 g, Saturated Fat: 3 g, Carbohydrates: 29 g, Fiber: 2 g, Sodium: 850 mg, Protein: 14 g

Spitting Paprika Chicken

Prep time: 5-10 minutes

Cooking time: 30 minutes

Servings: 4

Ingredients:

- Salt and pepper to taste
- 1 teaspoon garlic powder
- 1 tablespoon paprika, smoked
- 2 tablespoons olive oil
- 2 pounds of chicken wings

Directions:

1. Take the chicken wings and coat them with oil
2. Sprinkle with paprika, garlic powder, salt, and pepper
3. Transfer the chicken wings to the Air Crisping basket
4. Set your Ninja Foodi Smart XL Grill to AIR CRISP
5. Cook for 15 minutes per side at 400 degrees F
6. Once done, serve and enjoy!

Nutritional Information Per Serving:

Calories: 792, Fat: 58 g, Saturated Fat: 15 g, Carbohydrates: 2 g, Fiber: 0 g, Sodium: 721 mg, Protein: 62 g

Magical Coconut Touched Chicken

Prep time: 5-10 minutes

Cooking time: 12 minutes

Servings: 4

Ingredients:

- 2 large whole eggs
- 2 teaspoons garlic powder
- 1 teaspoon salt and ½ teaspoon pepper
- ¾ cup coconut minos
- 1 pound chicken tenders
- Cooking spray as needed

Directions:

1. Set your Ninja Foodi Smart XL Grill to AIR CRISP mode
2. Set temperature to 400 degrees F and set timer to 12 minutes
3. Take a large baking sheet and grease with cooking spray
4. Take a wide dish, add eggs, garlic, salt, and pepper, whisk well
5. Add almond meal, coconut and mix well
6. Take chicken tenders and dip them in egg mix, dip in coconut mix afterward
7. Shake any excess
8. Transfer the prepared chicken Grill, spray the tenders with a bit of oil
9. Air Fry for about 10-14 minutes until golden, serve and enjoy!

Nutritional Information Per Serving:

Calories: 180, Fat: 1 g, Saturated Fat: 0 g, Carbohydrates: 3 g, Fiber: 1 g, Sodium: 214 mg, Protein: 0 g

Herbed Up Roast Chicken

Prep time: 5-10 minutes

Cooking time: 5 hours

Servings: 6

Ingredients:

- 1 tablespoon pepper
- 2 tablespoon salt
- 5 sprigs thyme, chopped
- ¼ cup honey
- ¼ cup lemon juice
- 1 tablespoon canola oil
- 5 garlic cloves, crushed
- 1 whole chicken

Directions:

1. Add garlic inside the chicken cavities
2. Brush chicken with a mixture of honey, lemon juice, and oil on all sides
3. Season with salt, pepper, and thyme
4. Transfer to Ninja Foodi Smart XL Grill
5. Select Roast and cook for 5 hours at 250 degrees F
6. Serve and enjoy once done!

Nutritional Information Per Serving:

Calories: 280, Fat: 22 g, Saturated Fat: 6 g, Carbohydrates: 1 g, Fiber: 0 g, Sodium: 366 mg, Protein: 19 g

Wonderful Tangy Orange Chicken

Prep time: 5-10 minutes

Cooking time: 15 minutes

Servings: 4

Ingredients:

- 2 teaspoons ground coriander
- ½ teaspoons garlic salt
- ¼ teaspoon ground black pepper
- 12 chicken wings
- 1 tablespoon canola oil
- ¼ cup butter, melted
- 3 tablespoons honey
- ½ cup of orange juice
- 1/3 cup Sriracha chili sauce
- 2 tablespoons lime juice
- ¼ cup cilantro, chopped

Directions:

1. Take the chicken and coat them well with oil
2. Season with spices, let them sit for 2 hours in the fridge
3. Add remaining Ingredients: to a saucepan and cook over low heat for 3-4 minutes
4. Set your Ninja Foodi Smart XL Grill to GRILL and MED mode
5. Set timer to 10 minutes
6. Add chicken to grill grate, cook for 5 minutes, flip and cook for 5 minutes more
7. Serve and enjoy once done!

Nutritional Information Per Serving:

Calories: 320, Fat: 14 g, Saturated Fat: 4 g, Carbohydrates: 19 g, Fiber: 1 g, Sodium: 258 mg, Protein: 25 g

Easy Lemon Mustard Chicken

Prep time: 5-10 minutes

Cooking time: 30 minutes

Servings: 6

Ingredients:

- 6 chicken thighs
- Salt and pepper to taste
- 3 teaspoons dried Italian seasoning
- 1 tablespoon oregano, dried
- ½ cup Dijon mustard
- ¼ cup of vegetable oil
- 2 tablespoons lemon juice

Directions:

1. Take a bowl and add all listed Ingredients: except chicken
2. Mix everything well
3. Brush both sides of the chicken with the mixture, transfer chicken to the cooking basket
4. Set your Ninja Foodi Smart XL Grill to roast mode, set temperature to 350 degrees F
5. Select chicken mode and start; let it cook until the timer runs out
6. Serve and enjoy!

Nutritional Information Per Serving:

Calories: 797, Fat: 52 g, Saturated Fat: 20 g, Carbohydrates: 45 g, Fiber: 9 g, Sodium: 1566 mg, Protein: 42 g

Teriyaki Chicken

Prep time: 5-10 minutes

Cooking time: 30 minutes

Servings: 4

Ingredients:

- ¼ cup teriyaki sauce
- Cooking spray as needed
- Salt and pepper to taste
- 2 chicken breast fillets, sliced into strips

Directions:

1. Take the chicken strips and season them well with salt and pepper
2. Spray them with oil, transfer chicken strips to the grill grate
3. Set your Ninja Foodi Smart XL Grill to Grill
4. Set To HIGH
5. Cook for about 5 minutes
6. Flip and cook for 5 minutes more
7. Brush the chicken with teriyaki sauce and cook for 10 minutes more, making sure to flip once
8. Serve and enjoy!

Nutritional Information Per Serving:

Calories: 376, Fat: 25 g, Saturated Fat: 5 g, Carbohydrates: 3 g, Fiber: 1 g, Sodium: 1358 mg, Protein: 27 g

Italian Chicken Skewers

Prep time: 15 minutes

Total time: 25 minutes

Servings: 8

Ingredients:

- 1 lb. boneless skinless chicken breasts, cut into large cubes
- kosher salt
- Freshly ground black pepper
- 2 tbsp. tomato paste
- ¼ c. extra-virgin olive oil, plus more for drizzling
- 3 - garlic cloves, Minced
- 1 - tbsp. chopped fresh Italian parsley, plus more leaves for garnish
- 8 - skewers, soaked in water for 20MIN
- 1 - baguette French bread, cut into cubes

Directions:

1. Season chicken with salt and pepper. Make the marinade: consolidate tomato glue, olive oil, garlic cloves, and slashed parsley in a huge bowl. Add chicken and hurl to completely cover. Refrigerate 30MIN.

2. Preheat Ninja Foodi Smart XL Grill broil to medium-high. Stick chicken and bread. Shower with olive oil and season with salt and pepper.

3. Ninja Foodi Smart XL Grill broil, turning every so often until chicken is cooked through and bread marginally burned, about 10MIN. Embellishment with parsley.

Nutritional Information Per Serving:

Calories 260, fat 8g, carbohydrate 7g, Protein 38g.

California Grilled Chicken

Prep time: 20 minutes

Total time: 40 minutes

Servings: 4

Ingredients:

- ¾ c. balsamic vinegar
- 1 - tsp. garlic powder
- 2 - tbsp. honey
- 2 - tbsp. extra-virgin olive oil
- 2 - tsp. Italian seasoning
- Kosher salt
- Freshly ground black pepper
- 4 - boneless skinless chicken breasts
- 4 - slices mozzarella
- 4 - slices avocado
- 4 - slices tomato
- 2 - tbsp. Freshly sliced basil, for garnish
- Balsamic glaze, for drizzling

Directions:

1. In a little bowl, whisk together balsamic vinegar, garlic powder, nectar, oil, and Italian flavoring and season with salt and pepper. Pour over chicken and marinate 20MIN.

2. At the point when prepared to Ninja Foodi Smart XL Grill broil, heat barbecue to medium-high. Oil meshes and Ninja Foodi Smart XL Grill broil chicken until scorched and cooked through, 8MIN per side.

3. Top chicken with mozzarella, avocado, and tomato and spread barbecue to liquefy, 2MIN.

4. Enhancement with basil and shower with balsamic coating.

Nutritional Information Per Serving:

Calories 468, fat 23g, carbohydrate 38g, Protein 29g.

Sweet Chili-Lime Grilled Chicken

Prep time: 10 minutes

Total time: 2 hours 25 minutes

Servings: 4

Ingredients:

- ¾ c. sweet chili sauce
- Juice of 2 limes
- 1/3 - c. low-sodium soy sauce
- 4 - boneless skinless chicken breasts
- Vegetable oil, for the grill
- Thinly sliced green onions, for garnish

- Lime wedges, for serving

Directions:

1. In an enormous bowl, whisk together bean stew sauce, lime juice, and soy sauce. Put aside 1/4 cup marinade.

2. Add chicken to an enormous plastic sack and pour in the marinade. Let marinate in the cooler at any rate 2 HRS or up to expedite.

3. At the point when prepared to Ninja Foodi Smart XL Grill broil, heat barbecue to high. Oil meshes and Ninja Foodi Smart XL Grill broil chicken, treating with marinade until burned and cooked through, about 8MIN per side.

4. Season with held marinade and enhancement with green onions. Present with lime wedges.

Nutritional Information Per Serving:

Calories 340, fat 7g, carbohydrate 41g, Protein 26g.

Honey Balsamic Grilled Chicken Thighs

Prep time: 10 minutes

Total time: 1 hours 25 minutes

Servings: 4

Ingredients:

- 8 - bone-in, skin-on chicken thighs
- Kosher salt
- Freshly ground black pepper
- 2 - tbsp. butter

- 2 - tbsp. balsamic vinegar
- 1/3 - c. honey
- 3 - cloves garlic, peeled and crushed
- Canola oil, for greasing
- Chopped chives, for garnish
- Chopped parsley, for garnish
- Lemon wedges, for garnish

Directions:

1. Spot the chicken thighs on an enormous plate and sprinkle with salt and pepper on all sides. Work the flavoring into the chicken. Let sit, in the fridge, for in any event 60 minutes.

2. Then, make the coating: In a medium pot, soften the spread. Include the vinegar, nectar, and garlic and mix until the nectar has broken down. Season with salt and pepper. Set close to the barbecue.

3. Preheat barbecue to medium-high and clean and oil the meshes with canola oil. Include chicken skin-side-down and Ninja Foodi Smart XL Grill broil, flipping frequently and seasoning with sauce, until cooked through, 10MIN per side.

4. Present with lemon wedges and trimming with chives and parsley

Nutritional Information Per Serving:

Calories 440, fat 24g, carbohydrate 35g, Protein 21g.

Chapter 3: Beef and Red Meat Recipes

Delicious Cheeseburger

Prep time: 5-10 minutes

Cooking time: 15 minutes

Servings: 4

Ingredients:

- 6 burger buns
- 6 slices cheese
- Salt and pepper to taste
- 1 garlic clove, minced
- 1 onion, chopped
- 2 and ¼ pound ground beef

Directions:

1. Take a bowl and add beef, onion, salt, pepper, and garlic; mix well
2. Form 6 patties from the mixture
3. Press Grill on your Ninja Foodi Smart XL Grill and set to HIGH; select BEEF mode
4. Once preheated, transfer patties to the grill and cook until the timer runs out
5. Serve and enjoy by topping them with cheese and place them in buns
6. Enjoy!

Nutritional Information Per Serving:

Calories: 238, Fat: 17 g, Saturated Fat: 5 g, Carbohydrates: 6 g, Fiber: 2 g, Sodium: 465 mg, Protein: 16 g

Grilled Steak and Salad

Prep time: 5-10 minutes

Cooking time: 10 minutes

Servings: 6

Ingredients:

- Vinaigrette dressing
- 1 cup cucumber, chopped
- 1 cup tomato, chopped
- 4 cups lettuce, chopped
- Salt and pepper to taste
- 4 steaks

Directions:

1. Set your Ninja Foodi Smart to Grill mode and set it to HIGH, let it heat for 8 minutes

2. Season your steaks with salt and pepper generously, transfer them to the grill

3. Cook for 4-5 minutes per side

4. Take a bowl and add lettuce, cucumber, tomato and add dressing

5. Serve the prepared steak with salat

6. Enjoy!

Nutritional Information Per Serving:

Calories: 530, Fat: 30 g, Saturated Fat: 8 g, Carbohydrates: 15 g, Fiber: 5 g, Sodium: 897 mg, Protein: 50 g

Homely Honey Ham

Prep time: 5-10 minutes

Cooking time: 50 minutes

Servings: 4

Ingredients:

- 2 pounds ham, cooked
- 1 cup honey
- 1 cup brown sugar

Directions:

1. Take a pan and place it over low heat
2. Add sugar and honey, simmer cook for 10 minutes
3. Coat the ham with half of the sauce, transfer the ham to the Ninja Foodi Smart XL Grill
4. Set to AIR CRISP mode with the temperature set to 310 degrees F and set the timer to 40 minutes
5. Cook for 20 minutes, brush with more sauce and cook for 20 minutes more
6. Enjoy!

Nutritional Information Per Serving:

Calories: 239, Fat: 11 g, Saturated Fat: 6 g, Carbohydrates: 27 g, Fiber: 4 g, Sodium: 645 mg, Protein: 8 g

Bacon-Wrapped Up Pork Loin

Prep time: 5-10 minutes

Cooking time: 12 minutes

Servings: 4

Ingredients:

- Salt and pepper to taste
- 2 tablespoons vegetable oil
- 4 pork tenderloin fillets
- 8 slices bacon

Directions:

1. Take the tenderloin and wrap them with 2 bacon slices, secure with toothpicks

2. Brush all sides with oil

3. Season them with salt and pepper

4. Set your Ninja Foodi Smart XL Grill to GRILL and HIGH, timer to 12 minutes

5. Transfer the prepared meat to the appliance and cook for 6 minutes per side

6. Enjoy!

Nutritional Information Per Serving:

Calories: 462, Fat: 31 g, Saturated Fat: 8 g, Carbohydrates: 3 g, Fiber: 0 g, Sodium: 610 mg, Protein: 30 g

Italian Meatballs

Prep time: 5-10 minutes

Cooking time: 20 minutes

Servings: 6

Ingredients:

- Salt and pepper to taste
- 2 tablespoons parmesan cheese, grated
- 1 teaspoon dried Italian herb seasoning
- 2 whole eggs, beaten
- ½ cup milk
- ¼ cup parsley, chopped
- 3 garlic cloves, minced
- ½ onion, chopped
- 1 pound ground pork
- 1 pound beef, ground

Directions:

1. Take a bowl and add listed Ingredients, mix well
2. Form meatballs from the mixture
3. Transfer meatballs to your Ninja Foodi Smart XL Grill, select the Air Crisp mode
4. Cook for 20 minutes at 425 degrees F
5. Serve and enjoy!

Nutritional Information Per Serving:

Calories: 450, Fat: 27 g, Saturated Fat: 8 g, Carbohydrates: 28 g, Fiber: 3 g, Sodium: 1273 mg, Protein: 25 g

Different Pork Sandwich

Prep Time: 5 hours and 30 minutes

Cooking Time: 21 minutes

Servings: 4

Ingredients:

Marinade

- 1 teaspoon onion powder
- 1 clove garlic, minced
- 1 tablespoon fresh cilantro, chopped
- 2 tablespoons soy sauce
- 2 tablespoons lime juice
- 2 teaspoons cumin
- 1 ½ cups orange juice
- Salt and pepper to taste

Spread

- ¼ cup mayonnaise
- ¼ cup sour cream
- 1 teaspoon cumin
- 1 tablespoon lime juice

Sandwich

- 2 pork fillets
- 3 bell peppers, sliced into strips and roasted
- 8 slices French bread

Directions:

1. Combine marinade Ingredients: in a bowl.
2. Add pork fillets to the bowl.
3. Cover and refrigerate for 5 hours.

4. Strain and discard marinade.
5. Add pork to the grill grate.
6. Set the unit to grill.
7. Choose high setting.
8. Set time to 11 minutes.
9. Press start.
10. Mix the spread Ingredients: in a bowl.
11. Spread mixture on French bread slices.
12. Add pork to the bread along with the red bell pepper.
13. Grill sandwich for 10 minutes.

Serving Suggestions: Serve with pico de gallo.

Preparation & Cooking Tips: You can also use pork tenderloin for this recipe.

Peppers & Sausage

Prep Time: 10 minutes

Cooking Time: 18 minutes

Servings: 6

Ingredients:

- 1 white onion, sliced into rings
- 2 bell peppers, sliced
- 2 tablespoons vegetable oil, divided

- Salt and pepper to taste
- 6 sausages
- 6 hotdog buns

Directions:

1. Preheat the unit by pressing grill.
2. Set it to low.
3. Set it to 26 minutes.
4. Press start.
5. Coat the onion and bell peppers with oil.
6. Season with salt and pepper.
7. After the unit beeps, add the onion and bell pepper to the grill grate.
8. Cook for 12 minutes.
9. Transfer to a plate.
10. Add the sausages to the grill.
11. Cook for 6 minutes.
12. Add the sausages to the hotdog buns.
13. Top with the onion and pepper mixture.

Serving Suggestions: Serve with ketchup, mayo and hot sauce.

Preparation & Cooking Tips: Use whole wheat hotdog buns.

Beef Stroganoff

Prep Time: 10-20 minutes

Cooking Time: 30-45 minutes

Servings: 4

Ingredients:

- beef: 1000 gr
- onions: 500 gr
- champignon: 500 gr
- sour cream: 150 gr
- butter: 50 gr
- stock: 100 gr
- salt, pepper: q.b.
- paprika: 2 spoons
- flour: q.b.

Directions:

1. Insert the mixer blade into the tank.

2. Slice the onion very finely, then clean the mushrooms well and cut them into slices; finally cut the meat into strips about 5 cm long.

3. Put the butter, onion, mushrooms in the tub, close the lid, select the GRILL program, power level HIGH, set 40minutes and press the the start/stop button.

4. Cook for 15 minutes and then add the floured meat, paprika, broth, salt and pepper.

5. A few minutes from the end pour the cream and finish cooking for the set time; lower the power level if necessary.

Crusted Steak

Prep time: 5-10 minutes

Cooking time: 10 minutes

Servings: 4

Ingredients:

- Salt and pepper to taste
- 3 tablespoons parmesan cheese, grated
- 2 tablespoons olive oil
- 2 pounds flank steak

Directions:

1. Preheat your Ninja Foodi Smart XL Grill in AIR CRISP mode for 5 minutes at 400 degrees F
2. Take your steak and brush them with oil
3. Sprinkle cheese, salt, and pepper on top
4. Transfer them to the cooking basket, cook for 6 minutes per side
5. Enjoy once done!

Nutritional Information Per Serving:

Calories: 577, Fat: 37 g, Saturated Fat: 8 g, Carbohydrates: 23 g, Fiber: 8 g, Sodium: 688 mg, Protein: 37 g

Bourbon Pork Chops

Prep time: 10 minutes

Cooking time: 20 minutes

Servings: 4

Ingredients:

- 4 boneless pork chops
- Salt and pepper to taste
- ¼ cup apple cider vinegar
- ¼ cup of soy sauce
- 3 tablespoons Worcestershire sauce
- 2 cups ketchup
- ¾ cup bourbon
- 1 cup brown sugar, packed
- ½ tablespoon dry mustard powder

Directions:

1. Set your Ninja Foodi Smart XL Grill to GRILL mode and select MED; set timer to 15 minutes

2. Add pork chops to the grill and cook for 8 minutes, flip and cook for 8 minutes more

3. Take a saucepan and place it over medium heat, add the rest of the Ingredients: and bring the sauce to a boil

4. Lower heat and simmer for 20 minutes

5. Drizzle the prepared pork over the sauce and serve

6. Enjoy!

Nutritional Information Per Serving:

Calories: 346, Fat: 13 g, Saturated Fat: 4 g, Carbohydrates: 27 g, Fiber: 0.4 g, Sodium: 1324 mg, Protein: 27 g

Fleshed Out Onion Beef Roast

Prep time: 10 minutes

Cooking time: 30 minutes

Servings: 4

Ingredients:

- Salt and pepper to taste
- 3 tablespoons olive oil
- 1 tablespoon butter
- Bunch of herbs
- 1 bulb garlic, peeled and crushed
- 2 sticks celery, sliced
- 2 medium onion, chopped
- 2 pounds topside beef

Directions:

1. Take your mixing bowl, add the listed Ingredients:
2. Mix well
3. Set your Ninja Foodi Smart XL Grill to in ROAST mode and select BEEF
4. Transfer meat to cooking pan, let it cook until done
5. Serve and enjoy!

Nutritional Information Per Serving:

Calories: 320, Fat: 17 g, Saturated Fat: 4 g, Carbohydrates: 11 g, Fiber: 1.5 g, Sodium: 185 mg, Protein: 31 g

Fried Potatoes and Pork Cutlets

Prep Time: 20 minutes

Cooking Time: 30 minutes

Servings: 4

Ingredients:

- 1 onion, sliced
- 1 teaspoon garlic, minced
- 1 ½ lb. baby potatoes, sliced
- 1 tablespoon fresh rosemary, chopped
- Salt and pepper to taste
- 3 tablespoons honey
- 2 tablespoons mustard
- 1 cup breadcrumbs
- 4 pork cutlets

Directions:

1. Toss onion, garlic, potatoes, rosemary, salt and pepper in a bowl.
2. In another bowl, mix honey and mustard.
3. Spread honey mixture on both sides of pork.
4. Dredge with breadcrumbs.
5. Add the pork to the air fryer basket.
6. Select air crisp.
7. Set it to 390 degrees F.
8. Set it to 30 minutes.
9. Press start.
10. After 10 minutes, add the potato mixture to the basket.
11. After 10 minutes, add the pork on top of the potatoes.

12. Cook for another 10 minutes, flipping once.

Serving Suggestions: Garnish with lemon wedges.

Preparation & Cooking Tips: Pork cutlets should be at least ½ inch thick.

Bacon-wrapped Pork

Prep Time: 10 minutes

Cooking Time: 12 minutes

Servings: 4

Ingredients:

- 8 slices bacon
- 4 pork tenderloin fillets
- 2 tablespoons vegetable oil
- Salt and pepper to taste

Directions:

1. Wrap pork tenderloin with 2 bacon slices.
2. Secure with toothpicks.
3. Brush all sides with oil.
4. Season with salt and pepper.
5. Select grill function.
6. Choose high setting.
7. Set it to 12 minutes.
8. Press start.
9. After preheating the unit, add pork to the grill grate.
10. Cook for 6 minutes per side.

Serving Suggestions: Let rest for 10 minutes before serving.

Preparation & Cooking Tips: This recipe can also be used for beef tenderloin.

Grilled Steak with Dry Chili Dipping Sauce

Active Time: 30 minutes

Total Time: 30 minutes

Servings: 4

Ingredients:

- 4 - rib-eye or New York strip steaks, about 1½-inches thick
- 2 - Tbsp dark soy sauce
- 1 - Tbsp oyster sauce
- 1 - Tbsp light or dark brown sugar
- 1 - Tbsp plain vegetable oil
- 2 - plum tomatoes

Directions:

1. Combine the soy sauce, clam sauce, earthy colored sugar, and vegetable oil in a medium blending bowl. Coat the steaks with the soy sauce blend and let them marinate while you chip away at the plunging sauce.

2. Strip and deseed the tomatoes. Cleave the mash finely, and add it to arranged dried bean stew plunging sauce (Jaew); put in a safe spot.

3. Light one stack brimming with charcoal. At the point when all the charcoal is lit and secured with dim debris, spill out and spread the coals equally over the whole surface of coal grind. Set cooking grate set up, spread Ninja Foodi Smart XL Grill broil, and permit to preheat for 5MIN. On the other hand, set all the burners on a gas Ninja Foodi Smart XL Grill broil to high warmth. Clean and oil the barbecuing grate.

4. Ninja Foodi Smart XL Grill broil the steaks, turning every now and again until the ideal doneness is reached. Expel from Ninja Foodi Smart XL Grill broil and let rest for 5MIN.

5. Cut the steaks into ¼-inch cuts and present with the plunging sauce. Warm clingy rice as an afterthought is enthusiastically suggested

Nutritional Information Per Serving:

Calories 288, fat 11g, carbohydrate 3g, Protein 36g.

Memphis-Style Dry Ribs

Active Time: 1½ to 2 hours

Total Time: 30 hours

Servings: 4

Ingredients:

For the Dry Rub:

- ½ cup paprika
- 1/3 - cup dark brown sugar
- ¼ - cup kosher salt
- 2 - Tbsp granulated garlic
- 1 - Tbsp celery salt
- 1 - Tbsp chili powder
- 1 - Tbsp freshly ground black pepper
- 2 - Tsp onion powder
- 2 - Tsp dried thyme
- 2 - Tsp dried oregano
- 2 - Tsp mustard powder
- 1 - teaspoon celery seed
- ½ - teaspoon cayenne pepper

For the Mop:

- ½ cup distilled white vinegar
- ½ cup water
- ¼ cup dry rub
- 2 - racks baby back ribs

Directions:

1. For the dry rub: Mix together paprika, dim earthy colored sugar, genuine salt, granulated garlic, celery salt, bean stew powder, dark pepper, onion powder, dried thyme, dried oregano, mustard powder, and celery seed in a little bowl.

2. To make the mop: Whisk together vinegar, water, and dry focus on a little bowl. Put in a safe spot.

3. Fire up smoker or barbecue to 325°F. On the off chance that utilizing a vertical water smoker, for example, the Weber Smokey Mountain, place ribs on top rack with water skillet evacuated. On the off chance that utilizing a Ninja Foodi Smart XL Grill broil or balance smoker, place ribs over backhanded warmth. Cook until ribs have a slight twist when lifted from one end, about 1½ HRS for child's backs and 2 HRS for St. Louis-cut ribs, brushing generously with the mop each 15-20MIN.

4. Move ribs to cut board and brush with a mop. Generously cover ribs with rub and let rest for 5MIN. Cut ribs and serve right away.

NUTRITIONAL INFORMATION PER SERVING:

Calories 290, fat 23g, carbohydrate 4g, Protein 15g.

Chapter 4: Vegetarian and Vegan Recipes

Feisty Avocado Toast

Prep time: 5-10 minutes

Cooking time: 5 minutes

Servings: 2

Ingredients:

- ¼ cup tomato, chopped
- 2 slices bread
- Salt to taste
- 1 teaspoon lemon juice
- 1 garlic clove, minced
- 1 avocado, mashed

Directions:

1. Take a bowl and add avocado, lemon juice, garlic, salt, and pepper
2. Spread the mix over bread slices
3. Sprinkle tomato on top
4. Transfer to the Ninja Foodi Smart XL Grill and grill for 2-3 minutes at 350 degrees F on GRILL mode
5. Serve and enjoy!

Nutritional Information Per Serving:

Calories: 226, Fat: 15 g, Saturated Fat: 3 g, Carbohydrates: 21 g, Fiber: 2 g, Sodium: 267 mg, Protein: 5 g

Mexican Corn

Prep time: 5-10 minutes

Cooking time: 12 minutes

Servings: 4

Ingredients:

- 2 tablespoons lime juice
- ½ cup mayonnaise
- ½ cup sour cream
- 2 teaspoons garlic powder
- 2 teaspoons onion powder
- 1 and ¼ cups Cotija cheese, crumbled
- Salt and pepper to taste
- 3 tablespoons canola oil
- 6 ears corn

Directions:

1. Set your Ninja Foodi Smart XL Grill to grill mode, set temperature to MAX, and timer to 12 minutes
2. Let it preheat until you hear a beep
3. Brush the corn ears with oil, season with salt and pepper
4. Transfer to grill and cook for 6 minutes per side
5. Take a bowl and mix in the remaining Ingredients; mix well
6. Cover corn mix and serve
7. Enjoy!

Nutritional Information Per Serving:

Calories: 156, Fat: 10 g, Saturated Fat: 3 g, Carbohydrates: 15 g, Fiber: 3 g, Sodium: 163 mg, Protein: 6 g

Balsamic Tomatoes Roast

Prep time: 5-10 minutes

Cooking time: 5 minutes

Servings: 4

Ingredients:

- 1 teaspoon Italian seasoning
- ½ cup balsamic vinegar
- 1 pound tomatoes, sliced into quarters

Directions:

1. Take your tomatoes and toss them well in vinegar
2. Season them with Italian seasoning
3. Transfer to Air Crisping basket
4. Set your Ninja Foodi Smart XL Grill to Air Crisp mode
5. Set the temperature to 350 degrees F, and set the timer to 5 minutes
6. Transfer Brussels to the cooking basket, cook until done
7. Serve and enjoy!

Nutritional Information Per Serving:

Calories: 174, Fat: 14 g, Saturated Fat: 3 g, Carbohydrates: 12 g, Fiber: 2 g, Sodium: 11 mg, Protein: 2 g

Spicy Broccoli Medley

Prep time: 5-10 minutes

Cooking time: 15 minutes

Servings: 4

Ingredients:

- ½ teaspoon red pepper flakes
- ¼ cup toasted almonds, sliced
- 1 large broccoli head, cut into florets
- 2 tablespoons extra virgin olive oil
- Salt and pepper to taste
- 2 tablespoons parmesan, grated
- Lemon wedges

Directions:

1. Take a mixing bowl, add broccoli and toss with olive oil. Season with salt and pepper. Add red pepper flakes and toss well

2. Preheat Ninja Foodi Smart XL Grill by pressing the "AIR CRISP" option and setting it to "390 Degrees F" and timer to 15 minutes

3. Let it preheat until you hear a beep

4. Arrange a reversible trivet in the Grill Pan, arrange broccoli crisps in the trivet

5. Let them roast until the timer runs out

6. Serve and enjoy with cheese on top and some lemon wedges!

Nutritional Information Per Serving:

Calories: 181, Fat: 11 g, Saturated Fat: 3 g, Carbohydrates: 9 g, Fiber: 4 g, Sodium: 421 mg, Protein: 8 g

Super Garlic Potatoes

Prep time: 5-10 minutes

Cooking time: 20 minutes

Servings: 4

Ingredients:

- ½ teaspoon salt
- ½ teaspoon dried parsley
- ¼ teaspoon fresh ground black pepper
- ¼ teaspoon celery powder
- ½ teaspoon garlic powder
- ½ teaspoon onion powder
- ¼ cup dried onion flakes
- 2 tablespoons extra virgin olive oil
- 2 pounds baby red potatoes, quartered

Directions:

1. Take a large bowl and add all listed Ingredients, toss well and coat them well

2. Preheat Ninja Foodi Smart XL Grill by pressing the "AIR CRISP" option and setting it to "390 Degrees F" and timer to 20 minutes

3. let it preheat until you hear a beep

4. Once preheated, add potatoes to the cooking basket

5. Lock and cook for 10 minutes, making sure to shake the basket and cook for 10 minutes more

6. Once done, check the crispiness; if it's alright, serve away.

7. If not, cook for 5 minutes more

8. Enjoy!

Nutritional Information Per Serving:

Calories: 232, Fat: 39 g, Saturated Fat: 7 g, Carbohydrates: 39 g, Fiber: 5 g, Sodium: 485 mg, Protein: 4 g

Roasted Potatoes and Fancy Asparagus

Prep time: 5-10 minutes

Cooking time: 10 minutes

Servings: 4

Ingredients:

- Salt and pepper to taste
- 1 teaspoon dried dill
- 4 potatoes, diced and boiled
- 2 stalks scallions, chopped
- 1 tablespoon olive oil
- 1 pound asparagus, trimmed and sliced

Directions:

1. Take the asparagus and coat with oil

2. Season well with scallions

3. Set your Ninja Foodi Smart XL Grill to AIR CRISP mode and set the temperature to 350 degrees F; set timer to 5 minutes

4. Once done, transfer asparagus to the cooking basket, cook for 5 minutes

5. Transfer to a bowl

6. Stir in remaining Ingredients: and mix well

7. Serve and enjoy!

Nutritional Information Per Serving:

Calories: 222, Fat: 8 g, Saturated Fat: 3 g, Carbohydrates: 36 g, Fiber: 3 g, Sodium: 779 mg, Protein: 6 g

Cheesy Zucchini Love

Prep time: 5-10 minutes

Cooking time: 8 minutes

Servings: 4

Ingredients:

- 1 teaspoon olive oil
- ½ teaspoon tomato paste
- 1 zucchini
- ¼ teaspoon dried basil
- ½ teaspoon chili flakes
- 5 ounces parmesan, shredded

Directions:

1. Take zucchini and cut into halves, scoop out the flesh from them, and spread tomato paste inside the halves

2. Add shredded cheese, sprinkle with chili flakes, dried basil, olive oil

3. Preheat Ninja Foodi Smart XL Grill by pressing the "AIR CRISP" option and setting it to "375 Degrees F" and timer to 8 minutes

4. Let it preheat until you hear a beep

5. Arrange the prepared zucchini halves in Ninja Foodi Grill Basket, cook until the timer runs out

6. Serve and enjoy!

Nutritional Information Per Serving:

Calories: 300, Fat: 21 g, Saturated Fat: 1 g, Carbohydrates: 6 g, Fiber: 1 g, Sodium: 459 mg, Protein: 12 g

Lemon Pepper Brussels Sprouts

Prep time: 5-10 minutes

Cooking time: 10 minutes

Servings:

Ingredients:

- Salt to taste
- 2 teaspoons lemon pepper seasoning
- 2 tablespoons olive oil
- 1 pound brussels sprouts, sliced

Directions:

1. Take your Brussels and coat them with oil
2. Season the sprouts with salt and lemon pepper
3. Spread the prepared Brussels over the Cooking basket
4. Select the BAKE option, with the temperature set to 350 degrees F and timer set to 5 minutes
5. Let it cook, serve, and enjoy!

Nutritional Information Per Serving:

Calories: 229, Fat: 18 g, Saturated Fat: 2 g, Carbohydrates: 12 g, Fiber: 2 g, Sodium: 360 mg, Protein: 8 g

Spiced Up Chickpeas

Prep time: 5-10 minutes

Cooking time: 10 minutes

Servings: 4

Ingredients:

- Salt to taste
- ½ teaspoon cayenne pepper
- 1 teaspoon ground cumin
- 1 teaspoon chili powder
- 1 tablespoon olive oil
- 15 ounces chickpeas, canned, rinsed and drained

Directions:

1. Take your chickpeas and coat them with oil
2. Season them well with cayenne, chili powder, cumin, pepper, and salt
3. Transfer them to Crisp Tray
4. Set your Ninja Foodi Smart XL Grill to AIR CRISP mode, cook at 390 degrees F for 10 minutes making sure to stir once or twice
5. Serve and enjoy once done!

Nutritional Information Per Serving:

Calories: 182, Fat: 7 g, Saturated Fat: 3 g, Carbohydrates: 25 g, Fiber: 4 g, Sodium: 264 mg

Chapter 5: Fish & Seafood Recipes

Southern Catfish

Prep Time: 5 min

Cooking Time: 13 min

Servings: 4

Ingredients:

- 2 pounds catfish fillets
- 1 lemon
- 1 cup milk
- ½ cup yellow mustard

CORNMEAL SEASONING MIX

- ½ cup cornmeal
- 2 tablespoons dried parsley flakes
- ¼ cup all-purpose flour
- ½ teaspoon kosher salt
- ¼ teaspoon chili powder
- ¼ teaspoon onion powder
- ¼ teaspoon freshly ground black pepper
- ¼ teaspoon garlic powder
- ¼ teaspoon cayenne pepper

Directions:

1. Press the "Air Crisp" button on the Ninja Foodi Smart XL Grill and adjust the time for 13 minutes at 400 degrees F.

2. Combine the Catfish with milk and lemon juice and refrigerate for about 15 minutes.

3. Mix well the cornmeal seasoning Ingredients: in a bowl.

4. Pat dry the catfish fillets and rub with mustard.

5. Coat the catfish fillets with cornmeal mixture and transfer the fillets in the Ninja Foodi when it shows "Add Food."

6. Spray with cooking oil and air crisp for about 10 minutes, tossing the fillets halfway.

7. Dish out the fillets in a platter and serve warm.

Nutritional Information Per Serving:

Calories: 231, Fat: 20.1g, Saturated Fat: 2.4g, Carbohydrates: 20.1g, Fiber: 0.9g, Sodium: 941mg, Protein: 14.6g

Fried Prawns

Prep Time: 1-20 min

Cooking Time: 0-15 min

Servings: 4

Ingredients:

- Shrimp tails: 12pcs
- Eggs: n.2
- Flour: q.b.
- Breadcrumbs: q.b.
- Oil: liv.5

Directions:

1. Remove the heads from the prawns and peel them well.
2. Pass them first in flour, then in beaten egg and finally in breadcrumbs.
3. Remove the stirrer blade from the bowl.
4. Pour the oil into the bottom of the tub, close the lid, select the AIR CRISP program, power level 3, set 12min and press the program start/stop key.
5. Preheat the oil for 1 minute.
6. Add the prawns and cook them by turning them 2-3 times during cooking to even out the browning loa.
7. Serve accompanied with a jogurt sauce or mayonnaise.

Gouache Prawns

Prep Time: 1-10 min

Cooking Time: 15-30 min

Servings: 4

Ingredients:

- prawns: 800 gr
- lemon (juice): 1/2
- garlic clove: 1
- chopped parsley: q.b.
- olive oil: liv 3

Directions:

1. Wash and clean the prawns well. After drying them well place the prawns in a bowl and marinate them for about 1 hour pouring the lemon, oil, parsley and garlic.

2. Insert the mixing shovel into the bowl.

3. Pour the marinated prawns; close the lid, select ROAST program, power level 2, set 20min and press program start/stop key.

Mediterranean Sea Bream

Prep Time: 10-20 min

Cooking Time: 15-30 min

Servings: 4

Ingredients:

- bream: 2
- cherry tomatoes: 200gr
- black olives: 100gr
- garlic clove: 1
- thyme: q.b.
- salt: q.b.
- pepper: q.b.
- olive oil: liv 5

Directions:

1. First remove the scales from the sea bream; clean them, gut them. Salt and pepper the inside of the belly, add a clove of garlic and two sprigs of thyme.
2. Remove the stirrer blade from the tank.
3. Pour the oil into the tank and place the two gilthead seabreams.
4. Cut the tomatoes in half and pour them inside the tank together with the black olives and capers; salt everything.
5. Close the lid, select AIR CRISP program, power level 3, set 25min and press program start/stop key.

Air Crisped Salmon

Prep Time: 5 min

Cooking Time: 8 min

Servings: 2

Ingredients:

- 2 salmon fillets
- 4 teaspoons avocado oil
- 4 teaspoons paprika
- Salt and coarse black pepper, to taste
- Lemon wedges

Directions:

1. Press the "Air Crisp" button on the Ninja Foodi Smart XL Grill and adjust the time for 8 minutes at 390 degrees F.

2. Rub the salmon fillets with salt, black pepper, avocado oil, and paprika.

3. Place the salmon fillets in the Ninja Foodi when it shows "Add Food."

4. Air crisp for about 8 minutes, tossing the fillets halfway.

5. Dish out the fillets in a platter and serve warm.

Nutritional Information Per Serving:

Calories: 308, Fat: 20.5g, Saturated Fat: 3g, Carbohydrates: 10.3g, Fiber: 4.3g, Sodium: 688mg, Protein: 49g

Broiled Tilapia

Prep Time: 5 min

Cooking Time: 8 min

Servings: 2

Ingredients:

- 1 lb tilapia fillets
- Old Bay seasoning, to taste
- Lemon pepper, to taste
- Salt, to taste
- Molly my butter, to taste
- Cooking oil spray

Directions:

1. Press the "Broil" button on the Ninja Foodi Smart XL Grill and adjust the time for 8 minutes.

2. Rub the tilapia fillets with all the seasonings.

3. Place the tilapia fillets in the Ninja Foodi when it shows "Add Food" and sprinkle with cooking oil spray.

4. Broil for about 8 minutes, tossing the fillets halfway.

5. Dish out the fillets in a platter and serve warm.

Nutritional Information Per Serving:

Calories: 472, Fat: 11.1g, Saturated Fat: 5.8g, Carbohydrates: 19.9g, Fiber: 0.2g, Sodium: 749mg, Protein: 13.5g

Air Catfish

Prep Time: 5 min

Cooking Time: 12 min

Servings: 4

Ingredients:

- ¼ cup Louisiana fish seasoning
- 1 tablespoon parsley, chopped
- 4 catfish fillets
- 1 tablespoon olive oil

Directions:

1. Press the "Grill" button on the Ninja Foodi Smart XL Grill and adjust the time for 12 minutes at Medium.

2. Combine the catfish fillets with Louisiana fish seasoning in a bowl.

3. Place the fillets in the Ninja Foodi when it shows "Add Food" and spray with olive oil.

4. Grill for about 10 minutes, tossing the patties halfway through.

5. Dish out the fillets in a platter and garnish with parsley to serve.

Nutritional Information Per Serving:

Calories: 253, Fat: 7.5g, Saturated Fat: 1.1g, Carbohydrates: 10.4g, Fiber: 0g, Sodium: 297mg, Protein: 13.1g

Tuna Patties

Prep Time: 5 min

Cooking Time: 10 min

Servings: 4

Ingredients:

- 1½ tablespoons almond flour
- 2 cans tuna, packed in water
- 1½ tablespoons mayo
- 1 teaspoon garlic powder
- Pinch of salt and pepper
- 1 teaspoon dried dill
- ½ teaspoon onion powder
- ½ lemon, juiced

Directions:

1. Press the "Grill" button on the Ninja Foodi Smart XL Grill and adjust the time for 10 minutes at Medium.

2. Combine all the tuna patties Ingredients: in a bowl and make equal-sized patties out of this mixture.

3. Place the tuna patties in the Ninja Foodi when it shows "Add Food".

4. Grill for about 10 minutes, tossing the patties halfway through.

5. Dish out the fillets in a platter and serve warm.

Nutritional Information Per Serving:

Calories: 338, Fat: 3.8g, Saturated Fat: 0.7g, Carbohydrates: 8.3g, Fiber: 2.4g, Sodium: 620mg, Protein: 15.4g

Chili Lime Tilapia

Prep Time: 5 min

Cooking Time: 10 min

Servings: 2

Ingredients:

- 1 cup panko crumbs
- 1 lb tilapia fillets
- ½ cup flour
- 1 tablespoon chili powder
- Salt and black pepper, to taste
- 2 eggs
- 1 lime, juiced

Directions:

1. Press the "Grill" button on the Ninja Foodi Smart XL Grill and adjust the time for 10 minutes at Medium.
2. Combine the panko with salt, chili powder, and black pepper in a bowl.
3. Put the flour in one bowl and whisk an egg in another bowl.
4. Dredge the fillets in the flour, then dip in the egg.
5. Coat with the panko mixture and place the fillets in the Ninja Foodi when it shows "Add Food".
6. Grill for about 10 minutes, tossing the fillets halfway.
7. Dish out the fillets in a platter and drizzle with lime juice to serve.

Nutritional Information Per Serving:

Calories: 327, Fat: 3.5g, Saturated Fat: 0.5g, Carbohydrates: 33.6g, Fiber: 0.4g, Sodium: 142mg, Protein: 24.5g

Breaded Shrimp

Prep Time: 5 min

Cooking Time: 16 min

Servings: 4

Ingredients:

- 2 eggs
- 1 pound shrimp, peeled and deveined
- ½ cup panko breadcrumbs
- 1 teaspoon ginger
- 1 teaspoon garlic powder
- ½ cup onion, peeled and diced
- 1 teaspoon black pepper

Directions:

1. Press the "Air Crisp" button on the Ninja Foodi Smart XL Grill and adjust the time for 16 minutes at 350 degrees F.

2. Combine panko, spices, and onions in one bowl, and whisk eggs in another bowl.

3. Dip the shrimp in the whisked eggs and then dredge in the panko mixture.

4. Place the shrimp in the Ninja Foodi when it shows "Add Food."

5. Grill for about 16 minutes, tossing the patties halfway through.

6. Dish out the fillets in a platter and dish out to serve warm.

Nutritional Information Per Serving:

Calories: 246, Fat: 7.4g, Saturated Fat: 4.6g, Carbohydrates: 9.4g, Fiber: 2.7g, Sodium: 353mg, Protein: 37.2g

Chapter 6: Snacks and Appetizers Recipes

Chicken with Herbs and Cream

Prep time: 5-10 minutes

Cooking time: 15 minutes

Servings: 4

Ingredients:

- 4 ounces garlic and herb cream cheese
- Salt and pepper to taste
- 2 teaspoons dried Italian seasoning
- Olive oil as needed
- 2 chicken breast fillets

Directions:

1. Take the chicken and brush them with oil
2. Season them with salt, pepper, and Italian seasoning
3. Top them with garlic and herb cream cheese
4. Roll up the chicken carefully
5. Transfer them to the Air Crisping basket
6. Place the basket inside the appliance
7. AIR CRISP for 7 minutes per side, at 370 degrees F
8. Serve and enjoy!

Nutritional Information Per Serving:

Calories: 750, Fat: 42 g, Saturated Fat: 10 g, Carbohydrates: 18 g, Fiber: 3 g, Sodium: 846 mg, Protein: 73 g

Meaty Bratwursts

Prep time: 5-10 minutes

Cooking time: 12 minutes

Servings: 4

Ingredients:

- 1 pack bratwursts

Directions:

1. Preheat your Ninja Foodi Smart XL Grill in AIR CRISP mode for 5 minutes at 350 degrees F

2. Add bratwurst to the Cooking basket

3. Cook for 10 minutes, making sure to flip once

4. Enjoy!

Nutritional Information Per Serving:

- Calories: 739
- Fat: 57 g, Saturated Fat: 20 g
- Carbohydrates: 13 g
- Fiber: 3 g
- Sodium: 2641 mg
- Protein: 37 g

Delicious Taco Cups

Prep time: 5-10 minutes

Cooking time: 10 minutes

Servings: 4

Ingredients:

- 1 cup cheddar cheese, shredded
- 2 tablespoons taco seasoning
- ½ cup tomatoes, chopped
- 1 pound ground beef, cooked
- 12 wonton wrappers

Directions:

1. Press wrappers firmly onto the muffin pan
2. Transfer the pan inside your Ninja Foodi Smart XL Grill
3. Air Fry on AIR CRISP mode for 5 minutes at 400 degrees F
4. Top with ground beef and tomatoes,
5. Sprinkle taco seasoning, cheese
6. Air Fry for 5 minutes more
7. Enjoy!

Nutritional Information Per Serving:

Calories: 431, Fat: 21 g, Saturated Fat: 7 g, Carbohydrates: 30 g, Fiber: 5 g, Sodium: 604 mg, Protein: 31 g

Mustard and Veggie

Prep time: 5-10 minutes

Cooking time: 30-40 minutes

Servings: 4

Ingredients:

Vinaigrette

- ½ cup olive oil
- ½ cup avocado oil
- ¼ teaspoon pepper
- 1 teaspoon salt
- 2 tablespoons honey
- ½ cup red wine vinegar
- 2 tablespoons Dijon vinegar

Veggies

- 4 zucchinis, halved
- 4 sweet onion, quartered
- 4 red pepper, seeded and halved
- 2 bunch green onions, trimmed
- 4 yellow squash, cut in half

Directions:

1. Take a small bowl and whisk in mustard, honey, vinegar, salt, and pepper. Add oil and mix well

2. Set your Ninja Foodi Smart XL Grill to GRILL mode and MED setting, set timer to 10 minutes

3. Transfer onion quarter to Grill Grate, cook for 5 minutes

4. Flip and cook for 5 minutes more

5. Grill remaining veggies in the same way, giving 7 minutes per side for zucchini and 1 minute for green onions

6. Serve with mustard vinaigrette on top

7. Enjoy!

Nutritional Information Per Serving:

Calories: 327, Fat: 5 g, Saturated Fat: 0.5 g, Carbohydrates:328 g, Fiber: 2 g, Sodium: 524 mg, Protein: 8 g

Season Garlic Carrots

Prep time: 5-10 minutes

Cooking time: 10 minutes

Servings: 4

Ingredients:

- Salt and pepper to taste
- 2 teaspoons garlic powder
- 2 tablespoons olive oil
- 1 pound carrots, diced

Directions:

1. Take a bowl and toss the carrot cubes generously in oil
2. Season the cube further with salt, pepper, and garlic powder
3. Make sure that they are coated evenly
4. Spread the carrots in the Air Crisp Basket
5. Set your Ninja Foodi Smart XL Grill to 390 degrees F in AIR CRISP mode and set the timer to 30 minutes
6. Cook for 10 minutes, making sure to stir once
7. Serve and enjoy!

Nutritional Information Per Serving:

Calories: 183, Fat: 11 g, Saturated Fat: 5 g, Carbohydrates: 21 g, Fiber: 1 g, Sodium: 440 mg, Protein: 2 g

Sausage Patties

Prep time: 5-10 minutes

Cooking time: 10 minutes

Servings: 2

Ingredients:

- 1 pack sausage patties

Directions:

1. Transfer sausages to the Air Fryer cooking basket
2. Select the Air Crisp Mode and set the temperature to 400 degrees F
3. Cook for 5 minutes per side
4. Serve and enjoy once done!

Nutritional Information Per Serving:

- Calories: 228
- Fat: 13 g
- Saturated Fat: 5 g
- Carbohydrates: 5 g
- Fiber: 2 g
- Sodium: 145 mg
- Protein: 21 g

Cute Mozarella Bites

Prep time: 5-10 minutes

Cooking time: 8 minutes

Servings: 12

Ingredients:

- 1 cup breadcrumbs
- ¼ cup butter, melted
- 12 mozzarella strips

Directions:

1. Dip the mozzarella strips in butter
2. Dredge them with breadcrumbs
3. Add mozzarella strips to your Ninja Foodi Smart XL Grill Crisping basket
4. Cook at 320 degrees F for 8 minutes on AIR CRISP mode
5. Cook for 8 minutes, making sure to flip once
6. **Serve and enjoy!**

Nutritional Information Per Serving:

Calories: 206, Fat: 12 g, Saturated Fat: 5 g, Carbohydrates: 16 g, Fiber: 5 g, Sodium: 284 mg, Protein: 10 g

Simple Garlic Bread

Prep time: 5-10 minutes

Cooking time: 5 minutes

Servings: 4

Ingredients:

- Salt to taste
- 1 Italian loaf of bread
- 1 tablespoon fresh parsley, chopped
- ½ cup butter, melted
- 4 garlic cloves, chopped

Directions:

1. Take a bowl and add parsley, butter, and garlic
2. Spread the mixture on the bread slices
3. Transfer the bread inside the Ninja Foodi Smart XL Grill cooking basket
4. Cook at 400 degrees F for 3 minutes on AIR CRISP mode
5. Serve and enjoy once done

Nutritional Information Per Serving:

Calories: 155, Fat: 7 g, Saturated Fat: 2 g, Carbohydrates: 20 g, Fiber: 3 g, Sodium: 227 mg, Protein: 28 g

Particularly Crispy Tomates

Prep time: 5-10 minutes

Cooking time: 5 minutes

Servings: 4

Ingredients:

- Bread crumbs as needed
- ½ cup buttermilk
- ¼ cup almond flour
- Salt and pepper to taste
- ¼ tablespoon Creole seasoning
- 1 green tomato

Directions:

1. Preheat Ninja Foodi Smart XL Grill by pressing the "AIR CRISP" option and setting it to "400 Degrees F" and timer to 5 minutes

2. let it preheat until you hear a beep

3. Add flour to your plate and take another plate and add buttermilk

4. Cut tomatoes and season with salt and pepper

5. Make a mix of creole seasoning and crumbs

6. Take tomato slice and cover with flour, place in buttermilk and then into crumbs

7. Repeat with all tomatoes

8. Cook the tomato slices for 5 minutes

9. Serve with basil and enjoy!

Nutritional Information Per Serving:

Calories: 200, Fat: 12 g, Saturated Fat: 4 g, Carbohydrates: 11 g, Fiber: 2 g, Sodium: 1203 mg, Protein: 3 g

Fancy Baked Apples

Prep time: 5-10 minutes

Cooking time: 10 minutes

Servings: 4

Ingredients:

- 1 teaspoon cinnamon
- Zest of 1 orange
- 1 and ½ ounces mixed seeds
- 1 and ¾ ounces fresh breadcrumbs
- 2 tablespoons brown sugar
- ¾ ounces butter
- 4 apples

Directions:

1. Preheat Ninja Foodi Smart XL Grill by pressing the "AIR CRISP" option and setting it to "356 Degrees F" and timer to 10 minutes

2. Prepare apples by scoring skin around the circumference and coring them using a knife

3. Take cored apples and stuff the listed Ingredients:

4. Transfer apples to Air Fryer basket and bake for 10 minutes

5. Serve and enjoy!

Nutritional Information Per Serving:

Calories: 150, Fat: 5 g, Saturated Fat: 1 g, Carbohydrates: 35 g, Fiber: 3 g, Sodium: 10 mg, Protein: 1 g

Chapter 7: Desserts Recipes

Grilled Fruit Skewers

Prep Time: 10 min

Cooking Time: 12 min

Servings: 10

Ingredients:

- 1½ pints strawberries, sliced
- 8 peaches, sliced
- 1½ cups pineapples, cut into large cubes
- 3 tablespoons olive oil, for drizzling
- 3 tablespoons honey, for drizzling
- 10 skewers, soaked in water for 20 minutes
- Salt, to taste

Directions:

1. Press the "Grill" button on the Ninja Foodi Smart XL Grill and adjust the time for 12 minutes at Medium.
2. Put the strawberries, pineapples, and peaches on the skewers.
3. Season with salt and drizzle with olive oil.
4. Place the skewers inside the Ninja Foodi when it shows "Add Food."
5. Allow to grill, turning twice in between.
6. Top the grilled fruits with honey and serve well.

Nutritional Information Per Serving:

Calories: 132, Fat: 4.7g, Saturated Fat: 0.6g, Carbohydrates: 23.8g, Fiber: 3.3g, Sodium: 17mg, Protein: 1.6g

Chocolate Marshmallow Banana

Prep Time: 10 min.

Cooking Time: 5 min

Servings: 2

Ingredients:

- 1 cup chocolate chips
- 2 bananas, peeled
- 1 cup mini marshmallows

Directions:

1. Press the "Grill" button on the Ninja Foodi Smart XL Grill and adjust the time for 5 minutes.

2. Put the banana on a foil paper and slice it lengthwise, leaving the ends.

3. Put the chocolate chips and marshmallows inside the bananas and tightly wrap the foil.

4. Place the filled bananas inside the Ninja Foodi when it shows "Add Food."

5. Dish out in a platter and unwrap to serve and enjoy.

Nutritional Information Per Serving:

Calories: 137, Fat: 1g, Saturated Fat: 0.6g, Carbohydrates: 33.3g, Fiber: 3.3g, Sodium: 164mg, Protein: 1.6g

Grilled Donut Ice Cream Sandwich

Prep Time: 10 min

Cooking Time: 3 min

Servings: 4

Ingredients:

- 8 scoops vanilla ice cream
- 4 glazed donuts, cut in half
- Chocolate syrup, for drizzling
- 4 cherries, maraschino
- 1 cup cream, whipped

Directions:

1. Press the "Grill" button on the Ninja Foodi Smart XL Grill and adjust the time for 3 minutes.

2. Place the donut halves, glazed side down, inside the Ninja Foodi when it shows "Add Food."

3. Dish out in a platter and fill each donut sandwich with vanilla ice cream.

4. Drizzle the chocolate syrup on the donuts and top with whipped cream and cherry to serve.

Nutritional Information Per Serving:

Calories: 558, Fat: 27.5g, Saturated Fat: 13.2g, Carbohydrates: 70.9g, Fiber: 2.5g, Sodium: 310mg, Protein: 7.5g

Bloomin' Grilled Apples

Prep Time: 10 min.

Cooking Time: 30 min

Servings: 4

Ingredients:

- 8 tablespoons maple cream caramel sauce, divided
- 4 scoops vanilla ice cream
- 4 small baking apples
- 12 teaspoons chopped pecans, divided

Directions:

1. Press the "Grill" button on the Ninja Foodi Smart XL Grill and adjust the time for 30 minutes.

2. Chop off the upper part of the apples and scoop the core out of the apples.

3. Cut the apple around the center and insert narrow cuts surrounding the apple.

4. Put the pecans and maple cream caramel sauce in the center of the apple.

5. Wrap the foil around the apple and put the apple inside the Ninja Foodi when it shows "Add Food."

6. Dish out in a platter and top with vanilla ice cream scoop to serve

Nutritional Information Per Serving:

Calories: 407, Fat: 23g, Saturated Fat: 12g, Carbohydrates: 50g, Fiber: 50g, Sodium: 132mg, Protein: 4g

S'mores Roll-Up

Prep Time: 10 min

Cooking Time: 5 min

Servings: 2

Ingredients:

- 2 cups mini marshmallows
- 4 graham crackers
- 2 flour tortillas
- 2 cups chocolate chips

Directions:

1. Press the "Grill" button on the Ninja Foodi Smart XL Grill and adjust the time for 5 minutes.

2. Divide the chocolate chips, graham crackers, and marshmallows on the tortillas.

3. Wrap up the tortilla tightly and place it inside the Ninja Foodi when it shows "Add Food."

4. Flip the tortillas after 2½ minutes and dish out in a plate when completely grilled to serve.

Nutritional Values (Per Serving):

Calories: 429, Fat: 13.6g, Saturated Fat: 6g, Carbohydrates: 72.7g, Fiber: 3.3g, Sodium: 427mg, Protein: 5.9g

Grilled Pineapple Sundaes

Prep Time: 10 min

Cooking Time: 4 min

Servings: 4

Ingredients:

- 4 scoops vanilla ice cream
- 2 tablespoons sweetened coconut, toasted and shredded
- 4 pineapple slices
- Dulce de leche, for drizzling

Directions:

1. Press the "Grill" button on the Ninja Foodi Smart XL Grill and adjust the time for 4 minutes.

2. Put the pineapple slices in the Ninja Foodi when it shows "Add Food."

3. Flip the pineapple slices after 2 minutes.

4. Dish out on a plate when completely grilled.

5. Put the vanilla ice cream scoops on the grilled pineapple slices.

6. Drizzle Dulce de leche and sprinkle shredded coconut over the pineapples to serve.

Nutritional Information Per Serving:

Calories: 338, Fat: 9.5g, Saturated Fat: 6.3g, Carbohydrates: 61g, Fiber: 3g, Sodium: 101mg, Protein: 5.3g

Conclusion

The Ninja Foodi Smart XL Grill Capacity—grill 50% more food than the original Ninja Foodi Grill for delicious family sized meals. Grill grate fits up to 6 steaks, up to 24 hot dogs, mains and sides at the same time, and more

6 in 1 indoor grill—Grill your favorite foods to char grilled perfection, or go beyond grilling with 5 additional cooking functions: Air Crisp, Bake, Roast, Broil, and Dehydrate

Air fry crisp with up to 75% less fat than deep frying (tested against hand cut, deep fried French fries), using the included 4 qt crisper basket

The Ninja Foodi Smart XL Grill is, without a doubt, the best and ultimate option for your kitchen to serve a multi-tasking purpose of an air fryer, grill, pressure cooker, sautéing, simmering, dehydrating, and much more with just one simple and easy to use the device. You can easily clean the device as it is almost dishwasher safe except for the main unit, which should not be immersed in any cleaning liquid at all.

www.ingramcontent.com/pod-product-compliance
Lightning Source LLC
Chambersburg PA
CBHW080607170426
43209CB00007B/1357